Lucky Enough!

Poetry from a Life
By the Chesapeake Bay

By Deborah McGlauflin

> "If you're lucky enough to live by the Bay,
> you're lucky enough!"
>
> – A sign seen around Annapolis

Cover Photo credit: © Cappi Thompson | Dreamstime.com
Cover design assistance from Jocie Salveson

Copyright 2011 Deborah McGlauflin. All rights reserved, including the right of reproduction in whole or in part in any form.

Library of Congress Cataloging-in-Publication Data
McGlauflin, Deborah
McGlauflin, Debbi
Lucky Enough!: Poetry from a Life By the Chesapeake Bay

ISBN 978-1-105-04420-5

Contents

Spinnaker Sunset	5
Perfect Teacher	7
Things Change	9
Loblolly Pines in Three Scenes	11
The Bridge	13
Navy Show 'n Tell	15
Big Water	17
Bay Ghosts (four haiku)	19
Sailing Down the Moon	21
Beneath the Surface	23
Confession and Forgiveness	25
Jacob's Ladder	27
Annapolis Compromise	29
End of the Line (four haiku)	31
Slack Tide	33
In Season	35
Soundings	37
Lucky Enough!	39

_____

Dedication
About the Author

Spinnaker Sunset

Sleek yachts and daylight race apace
Downwind to the finish borne
Sunset's pastel reverie shattered
By gay neon sails and shouts that warn
By cheers and glasses raised to toast
Proud victors' due, the blaring horn

© Cappi Thompson | Dreamstime.com

Perfect Teacher

The Great Blue Heron
Doesn't know he is fishing
Alert eyes fathom the shallows
Without expectation
Suddenly a plunge of beak
Fish glints silver in alien air
A toss of head and plume
An undulent swallow
Then the still life pose resumes
Without goal or memory
A lesson in perfect mindfulness
Reflected in the still pond
To emphasize the point.

Things Change

The breeze clocks 'round and freshens
Laughing sailors spring to tend the sheets
Necks crane to watch the telltales flutter
All hands eagerly the wind shift greet

The tide goes slack and then reverses
The exposed concealed with each new flood
Just to resurface high and dry again
As moon's silent tug stirs Bay and blood

Ospreys return and build their nests
Battling eagles for fish with talons drawn
And horseshoe crabs of one sudden mind
All swarm the beach to mate and spawn

Waves wash the sand from shore to shore
Moving rhythmically with their reminder
Things always change and only change
And nothing could be kinder

Loblolly Pines in Three Scenes

Towering sentinels at the river's edge
A stand of loblollies drenched in moonlight
Silhouettes brushing the stars with scent

> Evergreen elders shoulder shifting winds
> Taller than passing masts on regatta day
> More carbon in their fiber and resin in their resolve

>> On a chill still tidewater morning
>> Loblollies float rootless on the mist
>> Serenely so and utterly beyond

The Bridge

Twin spans yet countless bridges cloaked in plain sight
Drenched in sunlight, rising from the shroud of fog
Raising high the motored din of restless yearnings
Five steel miles connect the bountiful Eastern Shore
And West's consuming appetite for more and more

Towering pylons touch the cloud-swept sky and plunge
Thickening downward through the ebbing flowing Bay
Holding fast to modern myth of stable bedrock
Tempered paths for water, rains to tides they weep
Grounding lightning to the darkest channel deep

From tidewater farms to faraway capital's tables
Summer corn makes grated peak on singing tires
Over watermen who haul the crabby feast
From dawn on tides' breath raking grassy shallows
Trawling slowly through the bridge's lapping shadows

In plain view hidden is the constant invitation
Past arching asphalt and behind the wheeling roar
To slow our headlong rush and note the sacred obvious
A binding web that steals the breath of all our suffering
A grace that soars beyond this time and place of longing

© Donald Conover

Navy Show 'n Tell

Sunrise over anchored "boomer"
Where the Severn meets the Bay
Tenders ferry Mids to visit
As they learn the Navy way

Awestruck faces all turned upwards
As Blue Angels shriek the sky
Thrills and chills of high-tech dogfight
Show the crowd what taxes buy

Brass returns to cheer the home team
Fly-by heralds game as war
Bill the Goat shows off the colors
Plebes with push-ups count the score

Parading smartly as the sun sets
Bugle sounds and flag descends
Making new the old tradition
The Brigade as one attends

Big Water

Glad again for twin engines' hedging bet
Limping home across familiar bay on only one
Gay plans dashed but all hands dry and safe
Time slows to a chugging crawl and starts to chafe

Pitching to and fro in newly noticed waves
Queasy passengers force smiles and ask how long
The captain rues remarks that passing sailors make
His gaze envying their smooth and silent wake

The crew on deck keeping a lookout tense
Alert for giants ghosting through the cloaking haze
Crossing the ship channel at Bloody Point with a shiver
Slow, but not in tow, making straight for the South River

Mid-bay seagulls bob and crossly screech
Herald freshening wind and day's fast fading light
Graybeard bay, rolling heavy now and dull,
Becomes big water, vast and menacing beneath our hull

© Donald Conover

Bay Ghosts (four haiku)

A path of crushed shells
Oyster ghosts' complaining shards
A crunch underfoot

    Once "Chesepiook"
    Explorers noted the name
    Algonquian echo

        Fossils on the beach
        Children squeal at ancient finds
        Where cliffs slough sharks' teeth

            Captain John Smith's trail
            Yellow buoys mark the way
            Past remains present

© David Neely | Dreamstime.com

Sailing Down the Moon

Cherished memory of that chill fall night
Teased from anchor by a beckoning breeze
Harvest moon pours out its ancient siren call
Loathe to lift a glass and end the season
Crew find all they need by way of reason

Enchanted eyes abandon charts and compass
The helmsman veers to steer moon's shining path
A "V" of geese in silent concert overtakes us
Flying low and parting smoothly 'round our mast
Their fleeting shadows grace the perfect spell that's cast

Beneath the Surface

Glaciers once receded slowly at their own pace
Not so today the underwater grass and oyster beds
Acres and acres gone fast missing, uncounted dead
In a silent losing war with the swelling human race

Beneath Bay's beauty and its lulling waves' roll
Algae multiply and die in smothering blooms
Creating dead zones which leave life no room
Out of sight and mind the grievous marine toll

Granddads recount with sighs a past that's lost
How as wading youth they clearly saw their feet
These days at times not safe to swim nor fish to eat
Their eyes reflect the sad and shameful cost

Behind the din that drives us nearly to distraction
Repeats the summons to awaken quickly and decide
Insistent moon tugs human blood as well as tide
And each dawn sun illumines what needs our attention

Confession and Forgiveness

In the autumn of my seaworthy life
I humbly confess the ever so now and then
Occasional bumping of Bay's ample bottom
I've known the silent wheeze of sloop's hull on mud
Escaped each time with a kedge or a quick tug
With no more than a red face to show for my lapse

I confess I've known the Bay's mercy
Shallow and shifting her channels, but forgiving
Gentle with her brackish tides and
Quick to release, shrugging off the insult
The lesson bobs unbidden to the surface
Whene'er my right of way is sorely wronged

Jacob's Ladder

Pilot climbs up Jacob's ladder
Scales the ship, commands the rudder
Safe to port in any weather
Guide through night and day

Steers a channel cut by glaciers
Keeps a course that clears the bottom
Ably captains any vessel
Mindful of the way

First to greet the world's seafarers
Moving trade in all directions
Up and down the busy sea lanes
Pilot plies the Bay

Every mark and every current
Etched in memory often tested
Passage true for dangerous cargo
Guardian of the Bay

© Deborah McGlauflin

Annapolis Compromise

"Isabel was here!"
Scribbled near a hip-high line
Sobering reminder on a shop wall
Monument to one battle in the long war

> *Locals know what tourists disbelieve*
> *City Dock is just from the Bay on reprieve*
> *Sandbags the inevitable only delay*
> *And Compromise Street admits water's way*

Ego Alley lies in certain wait
For hurricanes and spring floods
Waits to spill kayakkers over bulwarks
To paddle with the ducks among the parking meters

> *Only Alex Haley holds his seat, very wise*
> *Still reading to the kids while the waters rise*
> *Rooted Noah-like in the promise of a kinder day*
> *And the release of land from the grasping Bay*

© Herbert Quick | Dreamstime.com

End of the Line (four haiku)

Death by chicken neck
Pulled stealthily into air
Clinging crab is lunch

    Tired out watermen
    Sell the state their licenses
    Sadly haul their boats

        Old Bay-embalmed crabs
        Bushels to butcherpaper
        Fingers feel the burn

            'Naptown homecoming
            Retired officers play bridge
            By quiet harbor

Slack Tide

Sails doused and stowed, the anchor set in muddy bottom
Reclining crew rest tired feet up on the transom
Raised glasses clink as rose red sun's descent is toasted
Day's tales regaled, awash in evening pastels

The Bay stops drifting by the hull as now the tide slacks
Soon laughter fades and salty words lose their bravado
All hands content to rest in silence with the still creek
Unvarnished moment spreads across unvarnished deck

© Deborah McGlauflin

In Season

When the earth at last leans sunward
Spring things need witness by the Bay
Birds cued by longer light take wing
On brackish pond's rich feast refresh
Joyful journey's end those staying sing

Ears perk to hear the feathered din
Eyes note new shoots and greening trees
Nose tickled by the riot of rebirth
Rapt audience for returning raptors
My heart soars in season full of mirth

When the sun moves lower in the sky
And days grow short again I watch
Drunk squirrels leap and fill their cheeks
Songbirds grow plump and soon are gone
Empty osprey nests dot silent creeks

Leaves spread a carpet ankle deep
Then winter's chill descends and stays
On still pond and in bones that tire
Foxes find their dens and deer their thickets,
And I turn to tend a quiet inner fire

© Terrance Emerson | Dreamstime.com

Soundings

The hiss of waves' retreat on sand
The rusty "crawwwwk" as a heron lands
The lament of the Light on a foggy night
The honking "V" of wild geese in flight

The shot at regatta's starting lunge
The splash at end of an osprey's plunge
The clang of a mid-bay buoy passed
The whisper of wind in tall beach grass

The happy slap of tacking sails
The howling shriek of winter gales
The lapping of water against the hull
The lonely cry of a circling gull

By all these and more I know the Bay
Listen and love its sonorous way
When far away I go to sleep
I hear it still, its memory keep

Lucky Enough!

I'm lucky enough to live by the Bay
In an age when the glaciers aren't having their way
On a hospitable planet where much life has grown
Circling a star not yet nova in the Goldilocks zone
Protected by giants with their gravity's force
Amid spheres in polite orbits that cause no remorse
On a quiet arm of the Milky Way where less is more
Far from the swirling black hole at its devouring core
At a time when stars' light still fills the night sky
Indeed lucky to live by the Bay am I!

Dedication

This book is dedicated with love and gratitude
to my husband, Skip, who brought us
to Annapolis to live by the Chesapeake,
to his parents, Don and Jeanne, who kept coming back to
"Crabtown" and "The Boat School,"
and to my mother, Geneva, who joined us here and fell in love
with the Bay.

About the Author

Deborah (Debbi) McGlauflin is lucky enough to have lived in Annapolis, MD with a view of the Bay since 1995. She was born and spent much of her childhood in the great state of Maine, a place which is also near and dear to her heart and the subject of another poetry collection called *Maine Girl*. She has also published a third collection, *Getting Over Me*.

Debbi's poetry can be found online at:
http://mainegirl.net

www.ingramcontent.com/pod-product-compliance
Lightning Source LLC
Chambersburg PA
CBHW042324150426
43192CB00001B/39